Lots of toys can move.

Some toys move when you push them.

Some toys move when you pull them.

Let's find out how other toys move.

This hoop can move. If you push it with your hand it will roll.

This spinning top spins when it moves. Do you want to play with a spinning top?

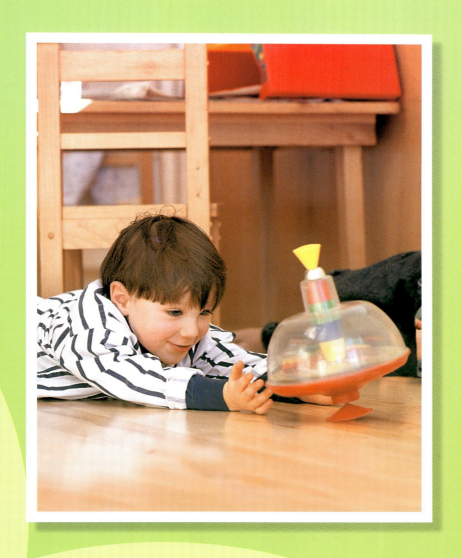

Yes, I want to play.

This kite can move. If you send it up in the air it will fly.

This robot dog walks when it moves.

Do you want to play with a robot dog?

Yes, I want to play.

This jack-in-the-box can move. If you turn the handle it will jump out of its box. This sailing boat floats when it moves. Do you want to play with a sailing boat?

Yes, I want to play.

This ball can move. If you throw it down to the ground it will bounce up again. Can you bounce a ball?

Yes, I can.